Going Back on
My Own Word
Selected Poems

Going Back on
My Own Word
Selected Poems

Andrew Marshall Jr.

Gotham Books

30 N Gould St.
Ste. 20820, Sheridan, WY 82801
https://gothambooksinc.com/

Phone: 1 (307) 464-7800

© 2025 *Andrew Marshall Jr*. All rights reserved.

No part of this book may be reproduced, stored in a retrieval system, or transmitted by any means without the written permission of the author.

Published by Gotham Books (March 14, 2025)

ISBN: 979-8-3485-8113-8 (P)
ISBN: 979-8-3485-8114-5 (E)

Because of the dynamic nature of the Internet, any web addresses or links contained in this book may have changed since publication and may no longer be valid.

The views expressed in this work are solely those of the author and do not necessarily reflect the views of the publisher, and the publisher hereby disclaims any responsibility for them.

In Loving Memory of
Mrs. Berniece Gary-Jones
AND Mrs. Elizabeth Himmel,

My BIGGEST FANS!!
They Knew TALENT!?

Mrs. Elizabeth Himmel
May 25, 1927 - March 19, 2024

Mrs. Minnie Mae Davis
June 10, 1935 - August 21, 2022

Mrs. Berniece Gary-Jones
February 9, 1935 - January 3, 2021

Table of Contents

Acknowledgment xiv
About the Book xv

Words That Sound Like Freedom 1
The Traveler 2
I Must Set History Straight! 3
Interpretation and Response 4
Rebel 5
Black People Got Sores 6
What Do You People Want? 7
Paradox 8
Without Cause 9
Just Wait 10
Inseparable 11
Hard Times 12
Last Minute 13
Elevation 14
Northern Hospitality 15
They Sing 16
Lights Off 17
Holding Down 18
Escape 19
Freedom 20
Color-blind 21
Three Tenets for Understanding Democracy 22

In Remembrance Of	23
Question with Nothing Answer	24
Nowhere Home	25
If We Are Not the Last to Laugh	26
Love	27
America	28
I Pray You Sleep Well Tonight	29
Along the Way	30
Old Shade Tree	31
What Hope Has the Race?	32
Memory	34
Prophetic	35
Eyes	36
Revolution	37
Tour for a Black Soldier	38
It is Written	39
In My Eyes	42
One Proud Nation of Prouds	43
Turning Point	45
Two Faces	46
Conscientious Divider	47
Praying Butterfly Prey	48
Synonymous With The "N" in NAACP	50
Hurricane, Eye	51
High on that Sun	52
The Life Love Left for Dead	54
Well-Watered Years	55

Openly Booked	56
Dust-off	57
Love Me With Your Lust for Love	58
Death Notice	59
Like a Water Breaking	61
Give Me My Flowers Now	62
Self-Medicating	64
My Sins Hasn't The Taste for Gin	65
Retolled2Death	66
WE The Feed for The FED	67
Lead Me But Don't Be Miss-LEAD	68
Beautiful, Children	69
The Making of Me	70
Luck	71
You, Too, is America, Too	72
Same Warning Against Your Other Warnings	73
Honeybee	74
Four-Leaf Clovers	75
Father to Daughter	76
The Great Fuss	77
Props Proper Properly	78
It	79
Fantasy	80
There is No Second Hand on the Ticked-off Clock	81
You are a Tomorrow's Baby	82
Pyromaniac	84
Stubborn	85

New Love	86
Caring	87
Commencing	88
Tainted Gold	89
Trapped	90
Censored	91
The Verdict	92
Overdosage	93
Unmasking	94
Your Knowledge Wealth	95
Don't Doubt the Prayer's Answers to Requesting Deferments	96
A Love Deferment	97
Ingredients for Love	98
Home Economics	99
Flamboyant	100
Heritage	101
Lone Soldering	102
I Pray for You, Two	103
To Hell with Aches	104
First Person Plural	105
Refund	106
APES Running Free	107
Count Sheep Before Falling Asleep	108
Civil Rights Movement	109
Conferred	110
Tap Dancers	112
Stir the Pot	113

There Was Always One Open Option Left Open After the Last Option Wasn't Close	114
So, Tardy of Time	115
US is Not "WE" Friendly	116
Beautiful	117
Stoned	118
Mother Furious	119
Not on Your Own Time	120
Complicit	121
To Hell with Nothing for All	122
Just Imagine What My Mule Could Be Doing	123
Punctuation Markings	124
Dashing	125
Window Shopping	126
The Black Set Back	127
The Word	128
Bridge	129
Generation Conflict	130
I Am That Man	131
Instead Of	133
Don't Break Your Stride	134
World's New Order	135
A Poem Signed "Anonymous"	136
Advice	137
Hero	138
Innocence	139
Nobody Loves Me	140
Forever and One Day	141

Mother	143
A Poem About The Black Woman	144
What I See When You Alone Dream With Me	145
Vision of a Future Past	147
Child to Father	148
In Remembrance Of	149
Black Love	150
Wish	151
The Lost Generation	152
Make Footsteps	153
Always Remember The Children	154
This Too Is Poetry	156
About the Author	159
Index	161

Acknowledgment

I am sincerely grateful to the following individuals. This book would not have been possible without their support and nurturing.

Bernard Gary, Michael Matlock, Patrick Bartee, Debra McGowan, former classmates and alumni at Bethune-Cookman College / University, for all of their continual support and encouragement. Bernard Gary provided unwavering support with his honest feedback and encouragement. My next collection of BIGGEST FANS!!!! ("4")

ALL of my siblings, enduring appreciation Mary N. Jones and Donald W. Marshall, who has been supportive in this and all of my other literary adventures.

Kimberly M. Quarles who has provided financial and artistic support during the completion of this book, along with making significant contributions toward other book projects.

Kenneth R. Davis, a valued friend and contemporary author who is always available to lend artistic and moral support and feedback, was also instrumental in the selection of poems in this book.

Teia G. Thompson who is forever supportive, encouraging and always objective.

Rhonda William so who was always supportive, encouraging and provided unwavering moral support.

Zeresh Gosha, my personal book coordinator, planner and organizer. Zeresh's insight and keen awareness is treasured.

Publishing team at Gotham, was totally committed to keeping me motivated and focused from the beginning to the book's completion.

About the Book

The book consists of a compilation of poems that the Author personally selected from his earliest, previously published books of poems. These poems that he selected for this book reflect the Author's personal favored poems. The book is a compilation of poems taken from the following books: The Keepers of the Shrine Poems, Words That Sound Like Freedom, Fire Burning Under Water, and Reading My Father's Will (there are two (2) books by this title). With respect to the books Reading My Father's Will, the Author designated these books his personal drafts to be edited at a later time. Subsequently, he did not attempt to promote either of these books. Consequently, there was minimal editing in the aforementioned books, except to correct a few little minor editing errors discovered in the books selected for this work.

Words That Sound Like Freedom

Words that sound like freedom
Are still up for sale,
So, you'd better enunciate them
Intelligently, as well.

Emancipation sounds like freedom,
But that never freed a living soul.
Emancipation is a proclamation
That someone else is in control.

Words that sound like freedom
Are synonymous, some might say.
You can protest and march to freedom,
But freedom is tricky that way.

People who want their freedom
Are all related, you know.
Some act very aggressively
While others move real slow.

Words that sound like freedom
Can make you act real dumb,
Like trying to hold a sacred feast
On somebody's discarded crumb.

But freedom is still revolutionary
And only the rebels are truly freed.
When you take back your freedom,
You will leave words to those who plead.

The Traveler

The Traveler journey shall last a lifetime along the way.
Even when travel plans aren't made
until after the traveler's destination day.
Other first-time travelers who were once curiosity-led,
Eventually dined with hunger while breaking Another off-bread:
"They will tell you exactly where to find your gold,
The hidden treasures that for yourself you must unfold.
The wisdom you seek is revealed from the inner side,
But to make this journey, you can break nearly a stride.
If going with the wind makes you slow down to play,
Then you mustn't wish that the sun rays would blow you away.
Best that you got your journey started this day, very early,
Because most travelers expire from the exhaust of miles of worry.
The roads that fork ahead is also paved,
With sparkling temptations that seduce the brave.
Your morals for such a trip you'll need,
Although this is one companion who steals like it's greed.
And the insomniac that cannot sleep through the night
Will now be awakened by the sound of a dimming light.
Do remember others as you continue on your path so straight,
Across the narrow bridges of those highways that bend but never see a (to) break.
Do laugh at life, but never belittle the youth in you.
Because you will end this journey with a prayer and the hope
That none of your dreams can ever be ruled or unruly, if true."

I Must Set History Straight!

I pay my dues,
Break no rules,
Make no excuse
For the man's abuse.

I must set history straight!

I tell it like it is.
Why should I let it be?
The way it has always been
For you and me?

I must set history straight!

I pay my dues
To sing the blues
The way I choose,
Win or lose.

Interpretation and Response

"I got an inching to call in the guards,
'Cause you Black folks are surely getting smart."
Call in the guards?
You won't have to go far.
The guards got radar,
They know where we are.

"You take my constitution and interpret matters;
You want democracy served on a silver platter."
Interpret matters?
That's what you say.
Democracy has been served
Forever that way.

Rebel

I ain't bearing a cross
For nobody, anymore.
The last time I had to bear
That cross,
Everybody else's soul was saved
But mine was lost.
On account of that, For nobody, anymore,
I ain't bearing a cross.

Black People Got Sores

Black people got sores,
Festering and full of pus,
A condition diagnosed
As terminal in most of us.

Black people got sores,
Like strays in a bed of ticks,
Whose master will never scratch
Anywhere near their itch.

What Do You People Want?
(Martin's Response to America's Question)

We want what you people want

And we want ours served judiciously in groves.

We want reparative legislation for

All of the inhumane sufferings of old.

We want you to uphold your tenets of freedom,

Removing the hood of peonage behind, which you hide.

We want all men and women to have decent jobs,

So, they may support their families with pride.

We want adequate training opportunities

When employment skills are lacking . . .

Echo:

Oh Lord, they hired and trained assassins!

Paradox

Disguised as a lamb,
My enemy stalks
In this land of honey
Where poverty is wrought.

With a glowing smile,
He is enraged with hate.
Being the last to judge him
Was my first mistake.

Without Cause

Love and hate encompass all.
I hate people who hate people
Without cause.

I love people who love people
When loving is good.

I hate people who love people
Who would kill if they could.

I love people who hate people
Within God's perfect light.

I love and hate with all my might!

Love and hate encompass all.
I hate people who hate people
Without cause.

Just Wait
(The Solution to Every Black's Problem)

If you people would just wait,
And in waiting you stay strong,
Maybe that would help the races
Make strides toward getting along.

If you people would not march up to
My White House with an ugly scene,
I would pass more civil rights bills
Than you could have ever dreamed.

If you people would just wait,
And in waiting remain very kind,
You will get all of this and more,
I swear I won't change my mind.

Echo:

If you people are just waiting
For bread to drop from the sky,
God ain't baking for fools
Who are just waiting to die.

Inseparable

Good news and bad news
Travel in a pair.
Find good news and
Bad news is there.

Hard Times

Times are hard and pennies are few.
Just don't know what I'm gonna do.
I've got a notion to cover the spread,
But my bookie might want me dead.
Nobody else could ever feel my pain.
Living is such a meaningless refrain.
Times are hard and pennies are few,
If you were me, what would you do?

Last Minute

Until the last minute
I wait to do most things.
I pray, then accept whatever
A day might bring.

At the last minute,
I covet, Steal, kill, and even hate.
I suspect at the last minute
Heaven will open her gates.

Elevation

Born colored,
Raised Negro,
Turned Black.
Now African-American.
Quit that!

Northern Hospitality

He was born in the South,
But migrated north on a tip
That he could escape the heat.
Although bigotry, hate, and prejudice
Shall follow him all the days of his life,
Northerners commend his plight.
In the North
Narrow-minded liberals smile,
And pose as friends.

They Sing

At ten o'clock
You were already too late
To sit in the pews where saints meditate.
Colored people's time did not come about
Until after the church first suffered drought.
Now they will wail for whomever
That might wander in.
Holy kisses have replaced
Repenting for one's sins.
Live bands play
And preachers fling.
"Nearer to Thee, My Jesus,"
They sing.

Lights Off

Death is rumored to be
Just like the life
I have always known:
Lights off,
Bill gets paid,
Lights back on.

Holding Down

I've been dragged through
The depths of hell,
Falsely arrested, but the judge
Denied me bail.
I've been accused of every crime
In your good and holy book,
Burned out of house and home
While the police just looked.
I've been called *nigger*
So affectionately until
I should change my name.
I've been fed bones under the table
For civil rights gains.
Yes, I've been dragged through
The depths of hell,
So, I can tell you the truth:
The devil's doing mighty well.

Escape

I saved my money
From my penny-paying job
To find that place far, far away.
I did not know
Where I was going,
But I knew I could not stay.

Freedom

Freedom is a mighty wicked foe,
Unless taken with force and fight.
Nothing sacred is ever given away,
When it comes from hands that bite.

Color-blind

Justice, they swear,
Is color-blind,
Without respect for what is mine.
Balanced on the scales of hate,
Her eyes are bound for her mistakes.

Three Tenets for Understanding Democracy

1

War is needed
Every ten years,
To help the economy
Get up the hill.

2

Some people know
The key to life
Is keeping the pie,
Never sharing a slice.

3

Believe in that
American dream,
Where people die
Or let freedom ring.

In Remembrance Of

Your keeper has a hobby of
Treating people like playing with soldering toys.
Indiscriminately he maneuvers
Old men, women, and young boys
All around the world
To make his living better.
He takes your life,
And buries you with his medal.

Question with Nothing Answer

When I FIGHT for RIGHTS
And FREEDOM and DEMOCRACY
And JUSTICE and ALL
Those other THINGS
That keep you LIVING
But KILL me QUICK,

What do I get?

Nowhere Home

I was raised in the South,
But the South was not raised in me.
So, I ventured out west,
Only to cowardly flee.

I hitchhiked to the North
(Where slavery had been abolished),
But the North was another South,
Just a few miles apart and hotter.

Back east I then fled,
To that color-blind coast.
But life was not as kind to me
As she is to most.

I moved only to lose
Because my thinking was wrong.
Being Black and in the center,
Nowhere is home.

If We Are Not the Last to Laugh

If we are not the last to laugh

Then we must smile and celebrate its meaning.

We must be glorified in the name and manner of

Our ancestors of ancient who knew the meaning of dignity.

They were determined to have the last laugh.

And they laughed so proudly and uncontrollably

Until they created what today is known as envy.

Such laughter freed their loving souls.

They laughed together and together they laughed.

Smiles were so free and, in such abundance,

That they were given freely to every brother and sister,

Then instituted as the standard for daily greetings.

Now knowing the origin of laughter and smiles,

If we are not the last to laugh,

Then our collective smiles must emancipate our souls.

Love

If love could
Enable me to go
Another day or two
And not be bothered
By the things that
Keep me awake
All night,
Then maybe I would,
Because sleep is good.

America

Where is your Black love that has died?

Has it died and just withered away
Like the corpse in an unmarked grave
Whose stench is now forever buried?

Is it quietly dead—
Knowing nothing—
And is soon forgotten?

Is it in a dead, slumbering sleep—
Blind and forgiving—
Divided and conquered?

Or has it been exhumed—
Somnolently sober—
Resurrected and united—

To utterly destroy,

By dealing wisely with you?

I Pray You Sleep Well Tonight

I believe in the kind of love
That is widely misunderstood.
I believe in the brotherhood of man,
Only when man's intentions are good.

I believe in life and liberty and
The inalienable pursuit of whatever.
I believe in you upholding your laws,
Their divine spirit, to the letter.

I believe in a true democracy
Where everybody has equal rights.
I believe in marching all day long,
Then pray you sleep well at night.

I pray you sleep well at night,
Because earthly peace is good.
I pray you sleep well tonight,
Eternally and forever, if you could.

Along the Way

Since they want to go to heaven
When they die,
They were told to love everybody.
And they would have made it, too,
Except they did not love themselves.

Old Shade Tree

When I can steal a moment for myself,
And lord knows I can't wait too long,
I'm going to behave like the whole damn world
Has packed its bags and just gone.

Then I will sit down on that rock,
Beneath that old shade tree,
And imagine the kind of life
Where my soul and troubles are free.

What Hope Has the Race?

What hope has a tired race
That is born comely and black
When they call upon the Lord,
And God does not answer back?

What meaning has a dream,
Reduced to ashes in flames,
When the dreamers must bear
Their oppressors' sinful shame?

I was despised before conception
And cursed in my mother's womb.
If Jesus is still the perfect bride,
Why would he seek a tainted groom?

I have truly loved everybody,
Since before the earth was formed,
And nothing more have I to show
Then a spirit broke from weathering storms.

Who can endure an infinite race,
From the beginning until the end?
When all the souls that hell rejects
Must qualify for everlasting life again?

What kind of freedom do I seek,
When my price for justice is life?

To inherit this wretched earth
Is a consolation that won't suffice.

To whose kind are we to be likened,
When none other has suffered so long?
Little comfort have we found in living,
Or the blasphemous instruction "Be strong!"

Why bother to judge the days of these people,
Whose lives, collectively, are just one minute.
What else could be their eternal fate,
When did the race begin without them in it?

Can what hope there is for any race
Be found in the duty of every man,
To live and die as you decree,
And always believe in the master plan?

But what hope has a tired race,
Conceived so Beautiful and Black,
When they shout the name of Jesus
And God then turns His loving back?

Memory

I'm not as dumb as I used to be,
Now I never forget a name or face.
And if I stop for a second or two,
I can recall the time and the place.

I'm not as dumb as I used to be.
Now I recall the time and the place.
And next time, like I promised you,
I will kick dirt in your *damn* face.

Prophetic (Malcolm to Martin)

Your death will be as violent as mine,
And you will be just as dead.
Whether you fall at the hands
Of assassins' bullets,

Or the man's apologists
Whom you gladly fed,
Your death will be as violent as mine,
And you will be just as dead.

Eyes

We are a race of would-be people, Expendable and broken,
With dreams that have died and dried up
Along the path of total annihilation.

Dear Brother,

You are the dreamer of my dreams!
You are held in slavery by my enslavement!
You are killed by my will to live!
You cannot escape the fate of
God's sunburned children you hate,

When you are a race of would-be people,
Expendable and broken,
With dreams that have died and dried up
Along the path of total annihilation.

Revolution

There will be no gentle breeze,
No picturesque sunset with standing trees,
No people to turn the other cheek,
No earth to inherit for the meek,
No justice for some but not for all,
No pawns to straighten your crooked cross,
No fear of that lesser enemy—death,
No mercy ever, until the last breath.

Tour for a Black Soldier
(A Poem for Kenneth Ray "Paco" Davis)

You must fight their never-ending wars,
To get your life's long disfiguring scars.
The fight isn't over who owns the land,
This is what some might misunderstand.
They quarrel over their slices of your pie,
If you wander, this is required to die.
I shot back and now must so gallantly flee,
The laws of the land are shooting after me.
Self-defense is not indefensible any more,
Death can't collect on its die 'til last *Gore*....

It is Written
(A Poem for Bernard Gary)

It is written that your people don't read.
(They probably can't read).
While being well-versed at being scared,
It's better to read than to be read.
They didn't read all about the Tuskegee experiments,
Or the systematic use of other agents of death,
Ensuring that they won't produce children to abandon tomorrow.
When your life is an open book,
You just write the stories they dare not tell.
You write them through your prayers,
And your incomparable faith in that second coming.
Just like there is strength in numbers,
If your wish is sincere, it might just happen.
"Lord, please send us another Marcus, Malcolm, Martin, Nat Turner, or John Brown."
Let's not be careful about what we wish for.
Sometimes it's alright to read what you have written.
Your people's plight is comparable to a mother's child-less womb.
You must read to them early for their incendiary development.
They don't know the right or wrong of it all,
Not until they are being read their rights.
Usually,
It is the right to remain silent.
Even the teachers placed them in a corner,
Backs up against the walls,
With the eight ball directly in front of them.

All alone their punishment was that of being forced to take out a book
And read quietly to themselves.
When they said,
"Read All About It,"
Black people were being economically savvy,
Saving for a rainy day, that is,
By deferring to read what little they could until later.
And later always pass you by, and you were home during the visit.
You hear it on every street corner:
"Nowadays, the news ain't nothing but the blues.
Besides, the damn papers have gone up two cents."
And those two cents plus the two cents you always adding
Becomes a catastrophic but Wall Street-like investment.
Yet Black people are quick to say, "My mama didn't raise no fool!"
Then they fail to understand the sacrifices that were made for you to
Go to school and one day change the rules,
By nullifying unkind Amendments.
You probably didn't read about your approval ratings, either.
They are the world's most stringent.
All killers:
AIDS. Hypertension, Diabetes, Homicides. Genocide, Poverty, Illiteracy, Anxiety, Bipolar, Cancer, Arthritis, Unemployment, Depression, Bad Credit. Mental Illness.
While being well-versed at being scared,
It's still better to read than to be read.
"All things come to the light,
When you read them in black and white."

Now, let every heart read between the lines,
Before your eyes start crossing them Ts.

In My Eyes

In my eyes there are cheers to life for going gray.
Got me clock watching love while time gets away.
When I am right or wrong it's the same either way.
Gonna take the rest of the rest of my last life back.
Gonna free Me some Me No matter where I am.
Got to see that Our People don't aim to get jacked.
Gonna move to a Place where the Sun does shine.
Wish to tempt temptation without crossing the dark line.
Want to *Drown* in true love while *Basking* with time.

One Proud Nation of Prouds

Women in drag,
Men in bikinis,
Why can't we sit down
And share a martini?

Women incognito,
Men in hoods.
From the looks of things,
This is not good.

Men and women
In thousand dollars suits,
Playing judges and juries,
And they took the loot.

Men and women,
Owners of the land.
People are starving
And they demand.

Men and women
Conscientious and free,
That's the only life
I want to dream for myself.

Men and women
Won't ever age old,

When a Nation's pride:
Being intolerable.

Turning Point

A turning point is when you had been pushed down,
After being forced to come all the way back around,
To the point you start again with another fresh frown.
The turning point is not unlike repulsive dissimilation,
Of a life that is never being completely above ground.

Two Faces

Sometimes,

each minute creeps and crawls,

then, mitigate a march to a crippling walk.

Extremely loquacious,

But never in earnest wishes to talk.

Eats your heart like the glutton who paces,

Then demands a second helping,

When disguised in one of its two faces.

Conscientious Divider

Conscientious Divider
The hate provider!
Conscientious Divider
The love crowds!
Conscientious Divider
Light to Dark rider!
Conscientious Divider
Dead-Killer-Spider!
Conscientious Divider
Slip-Slippery-Slider!
Conscientious Divider
Lies Speak Louder!
Conscientious Divider
Knocked-up outsider!
Weeping-lit-outrider!
Conscientious Divider
Wolf-Sweet-Cider!
Conscientious Divider
Heaven-Hell-Reviver....

Praying Butterfly Prey

One glance into *her-light-dark,* starry eyes
Revealed *his-hard-hearted* entire life story.
You could see the broken promises belying
That which was allure to a *One-Love-Glory...*

But beauty blames blank eyes that do not stare,
And life will recall a misstep made here and there.

Tormented by the ramification of a step or two
Missed along the way, with the ingrates faces sealed unto
Bad memories that time won't let time forget.
From waging on long-shot lovers never leaving,
Then placing a real sucker's bet on deferring your dreams,
Waiting for *unstubborn children* to not stub time's growth,
Finding laughter in tears that will not dry during decay,
Precipitating the death that will never get postponed,
Unlike tomorrow's guilt and regrets.
Practically begging opportunistic lovers, *disguised as physicians,*
To make timely rounds after having broken promises to administer *hope.*
To a dealer of life who perpetrates the butterfly's innocence,
No metamorphosis except love's blossoming fears.

Life takes on passengers who do not pay the fare,
Then makes beauty cross its eyes until they stare.

Beauty will barter with a lover's eternity:
She says, "I will give you my fortune for a little extra time,

Or, maybe, even my love's *timing-out* beauty for a generous fortune."

Still, Beauty remains the vanity of life's yearnings, although personified.

Still, Beauty was once a Butterfly that has now become the voiceless soul

That may only embrace the bleakness that surrounds her own mortality.

Beauty can barely bare the whispers of the judges who surmise about a life

Better off never revived to revisited. They, *the life judges,* will send another proxy,

Someone expendable and willing to announce the Butterfly's sentencing...

Having already pre-judged all of Life's mitigating circumstances,

Death is compelled to implore a reversal of mercy's contempt for mercy.

The sentiment being that beauty blames the eyes that do not stare,

Praying that vanity's vain will not berate a soul who has paid its *fare-share.*

Cause love's forgivings must recall a misstep or two made back there!

Synonymous With The "N" in NAACP
(Niggers Ain't Always Colored People)

MADE ALL of US in *differentiating* colors,
(this is non-controversial,
Indisputable fact, "Love.").
Give OURSELVES one of these
"*Desegregating Freedoms.*"
So *Integrating*!
Another Indisputable, god-fearing fact!
YOU will see nothing more than
The facelessnesses in YOUR twin's mirror,
When attempting to desegregate hate
for segregated fears,
While Proclaiming Y'all, too, is most *transparent*,
Posing *as the one good* "*BLACK!?*"

Hurricane, Eye

This eye of the hurricane,
Me and life's stormy ways.
The hurricane is in the Eye,
Moving time with the *grays*.

I am the I of the hurricane,
Flooding in gale-face wind.
The hurricane and I ignited,
As a *reaping sowing its Sin*.

High on that Sun (Shining)

High on that Sun,

Neither coming down.

High on that Sun,

Night *Blues* all around.

High on that Sun,

Too cold for heat stroke.

High on that Sun,

Memory startin' 'choke.

High on that Sun,

Hiding behind clouds.

High on that Sun,

Out, deaf-deadly *loud.*

High on that Sun,

Iminent returns.

High on that Sun,

Flat Line burns.

High on that Sun,

In stone, *inking.*

High on that Sun,

Closed eyes, Stilled,

And, also, sinking

At *The Last Drinking.*

The Golden Shovel

Underneath your lonesome and dead fir tree,
I planted a gift for you that now looks like me.
Somebody you might greet beyond the grave,
A companion to keep the golden road *PAVED.*
Dig not for the un-dug that cannot run nor hide,
Or *Cannibal* who eats living before *LIFE DIED.*

The Life Love Left for Dead

My plight is the same plight,
Journeyed by those who took
The road to the discovery of light.
All streets are paved with the gold of
Freedom's perceived possibility: Freedom Criterion!
My avenue, like the directions that are
Likings to the disliking of others,
Looking for the names branded on the engravers,
Forgiving the un-drippers of cooler waters at the feet
of the deserts' dusty hoarders.
But my name was always first on My list,
Since mine always begins with "a"!
Because *none* of the other walker-byes are yet to crawl....
Not too much further past home must a road endure endearing.
Were just as tired from chasing after
As is love from invading its own evasive

- Freedom.

Well-Watered Years

The Blinds are leading the Blinds,
And the Blinds are in the LEAD,
Following the HOLEY GRAYER,
Whose lit' children bleed of *greed.*

Openly Booked

Of course,
You know all about me.
My life is an open book.
I dance, sing,
Am a lovely avenger,
Can eat better than I cook.
Open the book of your life,
And, now, read nothing about me.
But I will re-bake in heaven,
Before hell resurrects and/or
Sets another dead soul free...to flee....

Dust-off

I've been dead all of my loving life,
And still don't know if I'll get to die,
Or should have died a darker grim,
Like living in the hollowering grave,
As life's pickings have gone too slim.

Love Me With Your Lust for Love

Love Me With Your Lust;
Forgive that I won't *Fuss.*
Love Me With Your Lust;
Toast me, but save *Crust.*

Death Notice

Got a little notice from Death,
And wasn't even on my sick bed.
Still got a notice, nonetheless,
That, in summation, said:
"I'll be dropping by to see you real soon....."
Just those opening sentiments nearly sealed my doom.
Read a little further and became distraught.
Death said, "Leave your lights on,
And I won't forget to turn them off."
At that exact minute,
I didn't have time for any unwelcome guests.
So, I gathered up all of my sins,
forgave myself, and just forgot what was left.
I'll forward Death a Change of Address,
Which really is the right thing to do.
Don't ever want to offend Death,
Do you?
I really hate to be inhospitable,
Even to an uninvited guest of mine,
Because Death and I have a longstanding invitation,
So, I'll catch Death farther down the line.
Just to let Death know that I was paying attention,
I told Death that I appreciate the self-invite,
But now my living is in remission.
Death can have the last word,
Which really is alright with me.

Should Death cordially invite me personally,
I demand that Death does *RSVP.*

Like a Water Breaking

The uppity souls escape to that heaven,
While breaking smoke from another hell.
Uppity people drink dry cupped up water,
But the *downers* hydrate and flood to *Jail*.

Give Me My Flowers Now
(Flatterings-Without-Flowers)

Give US our ashes now.
WE sell Your black coffins,
And buy down used caskets,
On *time,* All steals for frills.
Take from me Your strength
To push the swinging, singing
Chariot all the way back up the
Downthrottler's hill.
WE don't deserve to forgive,
While the hells are still burning up its congregation.
They just can't afford to wait for *thine* benediction.
The Pure Deaths *is* heaven-bound,
Willing to bet you've gotten one helluva detention.
Do give me my funeral now,
Before I'm no longer too young to go
Where I must re-raise my *dead-beatN("word up")-dead,*
Or can't Truly enjoy the *precipitating* death,
Like one who wasn't the toast for Your *Light-Bread,*
Cause Hell's once freezing life shall be
The fire that inflames my *overflowing burnings...*
Now out for my infectious LAST breath.
Give me my funeral now,
After y'all Come back and stay the *luck* away from my heart,
Always remembered for being up,
Then getting down like you *fin2* have another drink, on the House,
With the little gentle gentiles,

On the same paths that I, done, paved and walked with the *Love*.

Make the US crawl down hell's pyrite road in search of that Fool's *gold.*

Now when I cross my crooked eyes before you,

Let me show what is the truest deliverance: *UnforgivingLess*!

Heaven's *pretty-little-angry-angels*

Will return to heaven to SEE....

One Night WE all "will" (no more of the "shall" *Do! Do!*)

Inherit those *"Moody Blues,"*

After being drowned by the great swallowing,

Saving See! So End-WORD to its *Teacher(s)*:

Don't Forget about the US, but this here next time Do Remember WE!!!

Love Just Breaks My Grand Daddy Hard!!!

Echo:

Planted my sinning heart with a puncturing throng.

Now *Roses* will arrive with heaven's dead young.

Self-Medicating

You had to know that we were both sickly,
After all of the good years we have spent
Forever forgiving forever.
Life and living are an imbalance walk on, Water.
But now they have gone under, both of them drowned together,
Separately!
You must have hated your privileged, yet unearned life,
To leave love to suffer a precipitated last breath.
There are ills that will not hide with another bright lie,
And your sickness shall leave you a loner;
I'm minding the businesses of my diss-owned selves.
But when did you not notice that we are now dead?
Was it when the gentiles loaned that *Executioner*
Their Lord's sword that cannot pierce the skull bone of
The Wine-Maker's *Triple Sec Head*?

My Sins Hasn't The Taste for Gin

Who sinned-up my dreams,
On *sin* Dare?
Riding Me like the Night's a
Death Mare.
Pour ME once and I'll drink
Up again!?
OUR friendly, LITTLE Drunks,
Stirred-under, END-THEY-SIN.
The first to sink under the table
Dies with a drunkard grin...
In hell's hot sauced WATERS,
First *taste* of death's kickin' GIN.

Retolled2Death

We Sick *Love*!?
Don't you feel unloved too?
We are the slave driven to our own enslaver,
A death bill from the depths of
A new blew, *(C)old-mourning-heating*,
Yet cold's *dew, dew.*
We're all down here like brokenN-ones...
Looking like the plentiful just might overflow
And charge the hate back to you,
While your Numb of Dumb-de-Numb-de-Nation is
Blood's broken *throng* that crippled a kneeling *Hue.*

WE The Feed for The FED

Death is just the Good cup of *Pot Liquored,*
That goes down too slow for the inebriated.
Who lay on the ground after spreading legs,
Snapping the wishbone of hell's adulterated.
Death is not unlike the last meal for its dead,
Before sopping up the gravy with light bread.

Lead Me But Don't Be Miss-LEAD

My plight is a *TOLL ROAD*, too.

All roads lead somewhere,

'Cept that mine never seems to do.

Life gets longer by the mile,

And a lonely mile never travels alone,

Not if you don't subtract the falling, too.

I am willing to crawl all the way

To Heaven for free,

If you wouldn't have taken such long

BABY STEPS,

Throwing stones from Heaven,

After ME.

Beautiful, Children

The beauty of strength is immeasurable,
Like the infinity to whom beauty belongs.
The scent of your beauty is incomparable,
Just because your fragrance is never gone.

The Making of Me

First of all,
I'm sweet like that honey,
You love *taking* from the bees.
My eyes are wider than
Any river running into *love's* dreaded seas.
My soul feeds on the *meat* of the spirit,
From *mine* own ancestry,
Whose blood was sealed to *come* and *nonbondage* Me.

Secondly,
I'll take my seat at the table of Wise,
and wish only to out-live my *daydreams*;
Neither dying,
from the fears that the night might not survive.
Raised My standards higher than any incarcerating bars,
Forever *blessing* the heavens,
for redeeming *Another's* disparaging superstars.

Luck

Sometimes when luck do come your way,
You might just think *luck* is there to stay.
A gentle breeze from any People so tried,
Just might flip the *coin* to its *luckiest* side.

You, Too, is America, Too

MY America belongs to ALL America,
Not just the ones *shaded* for HIS hue.
Show that YOU do love OUR America,
Lest WE forget to remember the US, too.

Same Warning Against Your Other Warnings

You are smiling at me,
Like you are the one sitting
at the catbird seat.
But if you were truly ecstatic,
Your cages would be most neat.

You are laughing at me,
Like you are privileged
to watch from the *bird's* seat,
Stalking your prey,
Like a barren eagle in her heat.

You are rebuking me,
Like you are reclining
in the catbird seat. Waiting
for the children of the sun
To die from mistreated speech.

You are empathizing with me,
Like you are some kind soul,
Dancing on the catbird seat.
Like you aren't burning in hell,
And can't even *coldly* retreat!?

Honeybee

If you believe that I might ever run out,
Then you've got me mistaken for money.
May sting the stench out of a livin' death,
To keep flies away from its *sweet* honey.

Four-Leaf Clovers

The one thing you must do when you get on up:
Flood this wretched earth from Freedom's Cup;
Rain on hell with buckets of these *delish* tears;
Make your enemies regret his formidable years;
Pick grapes and raisins that the sunshine dried;
Give peace to death-ridden souls who ever tried;
Be the gluttonous comforter whose love *ran* over;
Let love replenish the earth with four-leaf clovers.

Father to Daughter
(A Poem for Raven Henry)

Lovely, don't you adore anyone

more than you love your own precious self.

You must live with you, when all others have left.

When man ravish you for your body alone,

miss him much, but let him stay gone.

Life begins with your consent;

teach the children about being President.

A virtuous woman knows no shame;

She can take the wild and make it tame.

The seed of your Nation

must pass through your womb.

A woman who is chaste chooses first

Among honorable grooms.

Always trust in a simple creed,

Like "Do unto others according to their deeds."

Believe in spirituality and do befriend thyself.

When all others have departed, love the ones that's left.

Let your undying faith unfold:

Honor your *Mothers* and *Fathers*,

and always keep your *Sisters* and *Brothers* close.

The Great Fuss

Black, Lovely and Tough,
Timber of the Great Fuss.
Gold is your loveliness,
Diamonds are your eyes.
None could have known,
But Your Creator, so wise.
Your spirit is infinite,
Like the wellness of calmed seas,
Comely and Beautiful,
With melanin flowing excessively.
The picture of antiquity,
Like an enduring masterpiece,
You have reservations
To live forever... and own eternity.
Gold is your loveliness,
Diamonds are your eyes,
You are bespoken,
By Your creation, So Wise.

Props Proper Properly
(A Poem for Tony Crawford)

Why didn't you *give* up on hope?
"Because my hopes done, come down,
up-on ("upon"?) me!" (that's *life* coming back unclear, not "US")
Now, I could have misunderstood
(and, maybe, even one day, accepted)
Your articulating something like:
"Hope gave me *up*!"
But, you said - "down!"
And you were expressing yourself
the *exactly* same and identifiable ways
Hopelessness be doing each time when He's coming around to
any one of *Our* one too many *Town*
(*unintentionally left off town pluralization, period*)

It (Burning)

If you are going to do it,
Then do it right.
You may do it in the daytime,
You might do it all night.

If you are going to do it,
Then do it with glitz.
The chances are great,
That You are going to do it.

If you are going to do it,
Then do it with a hot soul.
And do it right away,
Before IT gets *too cold.*

Fantasy

If you cannot fantasize,
Then dreaming is not wise.
A dream is worthy of dreaming
When your fantasies can be realized.
A fantasy is just a dream
With an element of surprise.
A dream loves fantasies,
Unless they refuse to compromise.
Your dreams can be so awesomely cool,
While your fantasies might dislike heat.
If your dreams should die to a fatal death,
Your fantasies will not wake and weep.
If you cannot dream of a fantasy,
Then your fantasies will not survive.
You cannot die from hopes of never daydreaming,
But fantasizing is what keeps those darker days in "*Surprise*!!!"

There is No Second Hand on the Ticked-off Clock

I Know how to handle a people when they get
Too much time on their little, untimely, idled hands.
One makes time stand ghostly still.
Like the way that only the watchful-eyed deviant doesn't understand.
Then when you start begging time not to move so fast,
That's when the time-preserved weathered soul has the last laugh.
Life doesn't stop to change its clock, even after it is broken,
Unless they tell you that today is the coming days ("latter days"), they have misspoken.
Why was I made to be the one not too tickly to tell the old time-gazers,
These are the seeds of your seed and they are all grown up from being lazy.
Now, guess what eternity didn't want the new clock watchers to know?
That freedom still moves at the same speed as its death blow.

You are a Tomorrow's Baby

I do worry about how old you are scheduled to be tomorrow, Tomorrow.
Sufficient for today is the factual that you get to flee your father, Yesterday's Tomorrow.
Giving no respect to that time for you to stop begging is what makes you a Tomorrow's Baby,
and a little Junior "*After-Hour-Kisser!*"
Bless your heart, cause very soon you will learn some crazy misnomers for "the deal."
Don't just take it from someone who took the deal (not Moi!).
Some are not offered the deal, while some accept the counter offer to the offer.
But you don't have to take the deal, even if you are the latest dealer unlikely to be dealing.
Tomorrow's Baby also is 'Yesterday's grand new "Old School."
Tomorrow's Baby will hijack the *good-darn* bus, if it's not going to or coming from night school.
But Tomorrow's Baby will not throw up from not having been silver spoon fed.
Tomorrow's Baby will love all colors, after seeing that Black blood is a darker red (blue).
Tomorrow's Baby must not be groomed to accept that *his-miss-coloration* lacks darkness
Effectively making you a percentage "Negro" (The most educated (un) and most God-fearing (without the sins) of his master's *beaus*.
Whereby, the old Negro was uh' confident and a wealthier boaster (again boosting).
and Tom lived hoping for a bluesy-eyed "tomorrow," for tomorrow

shall bestow upon him his "uncles" *hoodings*. If I may add a footnote here: Uncle Tom is a debit/credit card that won't be worth the salvation promised to you, if you can just wait and riot the day after "Tomorrow."

Pyromaniac

Gonna set my broken water afire,
Just to watch the afterlives boil and burn.
Gonna raise the stakes so much higher,
When I represent the pyromaniac's turn.

Gonna set the whole wide world on fire,
Until people live *together* or die in return.
The stench that rises to the mountain top,
The victory of death in the pyromaniac urn.

Stubborn

I want my freedom,
And I want it NOW!
I know about all of the hidden costs,
And I still want it, anyhow!?
God did pay for my resurrection,
When I dragged that wooden cross.
I had *almost* overpaid on my bill,
'Til that *receipt* got lost.
I want it now.
And yesterday shall have waited too late.
I want it,
Before another's freedom comes for me,
To spoil my own daring escape.

New Love

Find, compare, contrast, new love for the luck-lusting few.
They sacrificed and even compromised with love for you.
After re-mixing old pleasures with a youngster's new pain,
The two schools have become divided by lack of any gain?

Caring

How much does it cost to care any less?
Don't wish to short-change or forgive you.
Cause when I say my heart's now "Black,"
You immediately believe it's a Dark "blue."

Commencing

The innocence heart might believe that, squarely,

Education is a faltering nerd.

Trips to the library is often likened to a strong bull mating with,

A *convalescent* herd,

Never paying homage to the learning tree,

Instead, smoking and blowing away with its weed,

Would've been another "dope head,"

had it not been for hope being "brain feed."

To them, do say,

"Demand from life your highest best,

And do know that you alone

Must pass your own *addictions (or additional)* tests."

Tainted Gold

If the stars, ravishingly, impregnated the chastise moon,
Then lies with life and claiming to give the universe soul,
Who ages like fermented death soiling a path of tin gold,
That's too premature and living to be a postpartum, *soon*.

Trapped

Love can never dead-like die,
Killing life like panic runs slow.
Love may only rise up sky high,
Having nowhere else it can go.

Censored

I won't censor my lonely protesting self,
Cause I just don't have the loudest voice.
When it rains, then pours, 'fore flooding,
I was given only the *precipitation* choice.

The Verdict

No one is going to sleep through the last verdict,
No, not in the least of these darkened day times.
Some do indicate the faithful's right for a wailing,
While others are out for their constitutionalizing.
But ease the tensions of life's over-crowdedness,
Hotly, unlikeliness, anyone shall escape with hell.
Justice for all must become love's finalizing verdict,
As life collects on its percentage of a *complicit* bail.

Overdosage

I bet that my absence could never rid me of you.
I have endured more than you could have taken.
The signs of additions are obviously in remission.
They are the portraits of your faces lying at wake.
I regret that the world is a little less reprehensive,
That sinner You delivered from a temporal snake.
Misunderstanding the different degrees of venom,
Explains how you did make your first deadly escape.
So, let heaven rejoice from hell recycling a "Amen."
Consequently, a lie lives to the death of a post-complicit friend.

Unmasking

A *dead* deliverance
is only worthy of a *one-time*
forgiveness, for *your* friends.
But, N (now), the *doggone* meanest
will chase You all the way to heaven,
Just to integrate *his* version of your hell,
Repenting for *her* sins.

Your Knowledge Wealth

Your thoughts must flow coherently and continually,
In the crest of a new generation's hands,
As you encounter your "got to have."
Denoting a condition of one's respectability in this life,
Be it a woman, or be it a man.
People! Periods!
Equally non-negotiable is your latest harmonizing breath.
Then, neither dying nor death,
Could ever extinguish the fire in your knowledge's wealth.

Don't Doubt the Prayer's Answers to Requesting Deferments

I was awakened this morning,

By a misbelieving that today was yesterday.

My heart was then overflowed with love,

Some pity, but less than today's ownness of sorrow.

Now, I may celebrate before my living god,

Because that was the last time in my life,

I would die, just to see You ("again"!?) - *Tomorrow.*

A Love Deferment

Take care of YOUR love now,
And it will catch your falling off unto the deepest of ends.
Love THEE anyhow,
And none truer can you have to *befriend*:
Makes one feel like the adolescent who grinned.
Commune your heart's desires
In the languages that YOUR love doesn't misunderstand.
What is it about love that makes your heart
An over-worn-out welcoming mainstay?
Is YOUR love synonymous with life's "karma,"
Believing that you don't get what you did not pay?

Ingredients for Love

What are the ingredients for a healthy love?
Did you mix fear with your heart's sacrifice?
Or bake until it crusts like bubbles in crumbs,
Before tasting the flavors of the sweet dawn?

Home Economics

I learned my love of cooking,
in high school,
Because I could always see a vision of disobedience,
When told to put on *sole-less* shoes,
Jump into your kitchen,
fix me my *snacks on meal*,
Today!...
And you'd better not induce *labor*,
Along the *jammin'* way.

Flamboyant

"Flamboyant," is a fever in a crazy-acting Soul.
The eloquence of aging like forever,
All in just one identical day that never get to grow old.
"Where-about" sometimes you must *snuff-the-stuff* out.
The ones with the cash on hand,
Get to adventure around and about.
Flamboyant might mean, simply,
A tad of a *burden* at being always overdressed.
And only time will tell everything other than time,
Or whether this time's style stands the test of this time.
As much as it is a love of that fruit,
Forbidden,
as a privilege of the beginning and ending for any heart.
It's the prayer they continually Prays for the Praying:
"Lord, don't let those young 'Neanderthals' know,
We haven't ever been considered for having given a birth."
Flamboyant is an ugly, in addition, face-setter,
When it's the only "One" original attention-getter.
If I really had wanted to be the "most flamboyant,"
I would have, within time, committed a futuristic escape;
But I would not have bootlegged those "Little Richards" on CD,
When it was previously (formerly) "before a live audience" being taped.

Heritage

Some peoples disdain for you is so judgmental,
until they whisper that all of you look like y'all,
and that being from the all mighty "ghettoration."
But it is those same Ghetto attributes of yours
that make you come across like you is for real
and just might be *done* authenticating patience.

Lone Soldering

I've already had masking surgeries on my heart, soul,
And even my blinded eyes.
Must find a cure for being the first sacrifice,
Historically,
Who was deserted, and left to die.

I Pray for You, Two

Be very, very, somewhat careful,
With what you don't say to me.
I've been so under incarcerated,
Where life threw away the free.
Just be considerate of a muted day,
After losing one's denied freedom,
You never needed a worry to pray.

To Hell with Aches

Hell and Aches do become long-toiling,
Life's first tear as she stepped up crying.
They are life's heat strokes after boiling,
The migraine who remained after dying.

First Person Plural

We are the one!
We are the one!
We are the ones whose dreams are denied.
We are the one who decides if you've lied.
We are the ones, once we were lost from afar.
We were not invited, but, now, here we are.

Refund

They will not be giving out refunds,
So, for those who want their money back,
Stand at ready and willing,
Then cross your highway at the point of attack.
Some have not noticed that you have never been gone.
If you are not willing to live,
Then leave dying alone.
You might get a refund,
After they see who all is left.
Refunds are so inexcusable,
When you barter with your own, stubborn self.
Should you get your refund,
Blessed will be the lark for free.
But freedom that's placed on another's layaway
Charges a non-refundable and recurring and restocking, *Fee.*

APES Running Free

When someone uses big words on you,
you'd better know the trouble they can bring,
else you might find yourselves bleeding
from a wound that's deep and viciously mean.
Three-syllable words are enough for most folks,
Usually after that emotions are surely evoked.
Then you must read between the crooked lines,
what's ours is theirs but what's theirs ain't mine.
Know the difference between their uses of
synonyms, homonyms, and acronyms, too.
Synonyms are words that mean the same for others
but something entirely different for me and you.
Homonyms sound alike but have a different crease,
like receiving an invitation to your own last feast.
Acronyms are capital hate for your being in the world.
People abuse them freely, but they are simply absurd.
Once upon a time the NAACP would lend a hand,
Back then you were "Colored" not African American.
You must also be concerned with APES running free;
These are *Apologists Protecting European Supremacy.*

Count Sheep Before Falling Asleep

For some odd reason,
I cannot fall asleep
when counting hundreds (maybe thousands)
of white sheep jumping across my fence.
In fact, I am awakened by the scary thought of
one gentle lamb approaching my yard.
Anyway, I can't sleep when there is work to do.
I am compelled to chase them out of my life,
and far away from my home.
I got a wife and children to protect.
And besides, children must know the role of
the truly good shepherd.
Therefore, the children must be continually educated,
on the proper way to skin sheep.
Maybe then, after that, we can rest for a spell.
But I refuse to sleep until my people
fully understand the necessity of
counting sheep before they fall asleep.
You see, I don't want to dream that
someone pulled the wool over their eyes again.

Civil Rights Movement

People will sometimes look back on the sixties
and talk about the church bombings, water hoses,
marches, boycotts, protests, and cold jail cells.
It was cold how the builders of this great Nation
were paid with the Bills of economic deprivation.
Good-faith promises were made and dishonored until
cold-hearted politicians caught amnesia and just forgot.
Cold, cold, cold.

Is anybody hot?

Conferred
(A Poem Written In Memory Of My Parents)

My father would work at times,
By occupation he was a floater.
My mother worked night and day,
She was our life supporter.

My father didn't know the wages of death,
So in Jesus' name he drank to health.
My mother truly had incomparable faith;
She believed her man would eventually wake.

My father's plight I know too well;
White folks scared his soul to hell.
My mother bequeaths her living legacy,
A life deferred for my siblings and me.

Though time and time I cried for more,
Thank you for the riches in rags.
Only God knows the burdens in store
To prove the love of a Mom and Dad.

I truly love my father dearly now.
I understand his drunkard way.
I wish to kiss my mother somehow
And give her back that deferred pay.

There is hope in being my mother's child,
But my father I more strongly resemble,

Since the keepers of this world defiled
My being a man and a status symbol.

What reason does a child have to dream,
When all his dreams have been revoked?
And where is the joy that living brings,
After both parents die from stroke?

Tap Dancers

Black People got happy feet,
Moving to a syncopated beat.
Life guises with its bronze grin.
Music is never jazzy when
Breaking new shoes in.

Catch your steady beat,
Wear shoes that city sweeps,
Stand your soulful meek,
Dig life that's muddy deep,
'Cause rain floods little black feet.

Rain floods little black feet!

Stir the Pot

You may call me black,
But don't call me blue.
It's better than "Toby"?
Why, that isn't so true!

You may call me blue,
But don't call me black.
I've searched the world,
No other rhyme like that.

You may call me black
And add shades of blue.
Death shall beg forgiveness,
After making a *darky stew*.

There Was Always One Open Option Left Open After the Last Option Wasn't Close

Instead of resolving this tongue-twisting *mad-cow-manure* (*"Best Served"*),

I'd rather pull the proverbial trigger.

Cause *MY* headlines will still read:

"Another Death for *That Homelessness Figure.*"

Twisted, proverbial, and surreal.

This must be the way,

Finalizing dying all at once must ("gonna") feel!?

But instead of bargaining to cleanse the dirty *river's soul*,

Discover why his coldness, bloodiness,

Makes the warmest heart shiver in the face of silverised gold.

Or, why not ask anyone who knows about choking

On a swallowed pride!?

Because they might not have to deliver to the People

That death is to the oppressor,

What a lost love is to the oppressed,

After being blessedly committed to one's own *temporary* suicide.

So, Tardy of Time

Time used to be too early,
Now, time is never, actually, running late.
If I weren't having those clock-stopping clues,
Time would serve the longest detention,
After braking with standard waiting rules.
Time would get marked "Tardy,"
Absent a late midnight protest.
And, if you find your lost time tomorrow,
You may sleep by the clock,
Cause that last time,
You must've stopped for *piece-of-rest.*

US is Not "WE" Friendly

You and I are not "US" friendly,
And the whole wide world was
once in your hands,
Having, independently, concluded
the reconciliation of a bronze fact:
Since death is a reprieve from the sun,
You are going to see that a segregated hell
Wasn't integrated just for the *jetting* Black.

Beautiful (or "Incomparable")

Your beauty is the eyes that un-shames my soul.
And, of course, my love is much appreciative of this.
If the journey to paradise is rose pedaled with gold,
Then love has granted the open-hearted "the" wish.
You are the unparalleled companion who flaunts,
between Virtuous beauty and a Comely endeavor.
You are the reflection of a Merciful Creation,
Whose arms reach out to hold love's beauty - forever.

Stoned

For the remainder of the rest of my life,
I'll never get to live the same way again.
In celebration of *these* accomplishment,
I will throw the ceremonial first stone...
Into a great BIG bucket of my *owned* sin.

Mother Furious

I hate all of my days equally,
Cause each one of their passing
Could've given birth to freedom.
To hate one more than the other,
Would and suggest that this day,
Haven't set my fool-self free of You.

Not on Your Own Time

You may have been right about the others,
Mostly, all of the other times,
Without protest or exception,
But you are still just a "little-right" today.
Those Coloreds have placed a bounty on your *un-interest,*
Posthumously renamed after "Back" and "Pay."
Your "righteous" earnings for disinterest and hate-compounded,
Equates to hefty, bloody thirsting, fines.
As a prelude,
Death shall exhume the spiritless,
Cause you will never truly rest in peace,
During the loveliest of your *down time.*

Complicit

Don't taint my polluted water,
Then call yourselves baptizing me.
My Soul has proclaimed,
"Water runs smoother when I am free!"
Don't doubt your deliverance in prayer,
But I, now, am refusing to beg.
You do know that that devil kicked at you,
With what might be between their legs.
Who else would bite a black apple just to slither away?
In spite of all of the risks,
To whom is the right way to pray?
Who should be that redeemer,
Who intercepts on my behalf?
And,
When forgiving for sin,
I must give that *Postponement Day* a pass?

To Hell with Nothing for All

How much less do you need?
You don't have to give life an exact amount.
Just make it slightly higher than
Being above what forgiveness didn't count.
That's about three fifths of heaven's lot,
Which is still less than what the *deafs* got.

Just Imagine What My Mule Could Be Doing ("Pushing")

Image the ones who have crossed over,
And have seen the promised land.
Imagine that they will forever love you more
Then your *beneficiaries* can.
Imagine seeing the promised land,
While dragging the benefactors by their knee,
Then try loving a wide-eyed capitalist who cannot see.
(For some, who still want it all.)
Imagine working 40 acres with a gift mule:
Knowing that you will never open his eyes,
Until you quit pulling his lazy *ass*.

Punctuation Markings

Whenever you are sure of the punctuation,
You may use a period.
A period also comes in handy,
(Particularly, when you are unready to have a stillbirth).
A period can denote a foppish to catch one's breath,
Which should be the last sign to be coming first.
There may be multiple misuses of a punctuation,
Before your story ends.
But an "exclamation mark" may connote that
Those who are last to laugh,
May start smiling boldly again!?

Dashing

When I dress up to lay down,
And face that forever,
Don't want no fanfare.
Knowing me not as well as once I did,
I'd return to the *bull shunned* dare.
Cause until their moment to confront to the extent,
The sins of living weren't only for a lying repent.
The wages of sin mean you get left.
So forever isn't child's play,
Like the repentance game itself.
When you lay down forever,
Missing days cannot be returned.
When you lay down forever,
All learning has been learned.
When you lay down forever,
No more sleeping on the job.
It will take forever, minimally,
To infiltrate the heavens with
A *flashing* mob.

Window Shopping

You once loved the denotation - "simultaneously,"
So, now you owe hell,
Because they are both multi-tasking,
And all on insanity's insane excess,
Freed away from time.
Before, the "My, how they have grown!?"
The minds were idling very well,
And, also, finely *N("NEWLY")*-tuned.

The Black Set Back

"The Black set back,"
Sounds like a breaking point in an olden confirmation,
You might want "lyricized" in your redemptive song.
It also could be one path towards that alarming headache,
Ringing on the outside of your inner ear.
The enchanting chorus harmonizing,
"Lover, Which Death Do You Not Fear?"
But yours is the most multi-rhythmic,
Uni-motivational song.
Know that Black time can be killed,
From violently crawling on the straight and narrow,
Or resting peacefully before being *hung*.

The Word

Believing is seeing the greatest *Literary of Sciences*,
Since becoming the revolutionary Biblical.
But the "word" must be that of the creator,
(And only one creator is entitled, per creation!?)
But to those who know the wording. truths are humbly reserved.
Why does envy withhold beauty from its own "casted out" rest!?
Write what you like about disentitlement,
But scribe your inalienable, remarked best.
Don't tell yourselves the lying truth,
To advance to the pain of denial,
When the purpose of redemptive living,
Should be to wear the crown of "foolproof,"
After re-claiming re-birth *before* re-dying.

Bridge

How do you build your loving bridge?
Is it sky high over bubbling, hot water?
Since love is the wisest of all Engineers,
Love has an imperfectly pecking order.
Love cannot be that plight-less Soldier,
Stealing the children's lifetime of kisses.
True Love master builder most beautiful,
Mending hearts to call heaven a reward.

Generation Conflict

Men of goodwill,
Grounded in the times of old,
Could take a lone loaf of bread
And abundantly feed the masses.

But today the children would rather feast
On the crumbs gathered during the revolution,
Because bread alone is unacceptable.

I Am That Man
(The Pledge of a Man)

I take responsibility for all of my own actions,
While steadfastly remaining my brothers' keeper.
My blood is as ancient as the mighty Nile River;
The depths of my heart and soul are even deeper.

My conscience will guide life's path and direction,
And a true understanding shall accompany the faith.
Since no man has arrived until his People get there,
If they take forever and a day, I would patiently wait.

I Am That Man

I will make no apologies for my beloved blackness,
Although I might sing and dance like I am possessed.
I know the truth regarding the things that matter most,
So I don't give a damn about failing your biased tests.

I provide for my family and protect their interests,
Like a comforter sent from their merciful God.
Should someone disrespect or violate my house rules,
I will precipitate the coming of their eternal reward.

I Am That Man

Some may look at me with astonishment and wonder,
Who in this earthly hell do I really believe I am.
Because I have set my own self incorruptibly free,
I am not subjected to anyone's treacherous demands.

I am the honorable Man of Alpha and Omega ancestry,
And I must rewrite my history in this foreign land.
When the first ship set sail by astrological light,
I am He who guided the rudder with his Black hands.

I Am That Man

I seek delight in whatsoever changes a day might bring,
And I am compelled to make right wrongs as they unfold.
Nothing will ever stop my pursuit of Truth and Justice,
And never will I compromise by selling my People's soul

I will stand firm and walk erect with pride and dignity,
Because this man has backbone and does not beg nor bow.
Then if I don't live to see tomorrow's glorious sunset,
I shall die knowing that my living was truly worthwhile.

Instead Of

I will drag my feet,
Instead of
Stretching forth both my legs and walking.

I will bite my tongue,
Instead of
Opening my mouth wide and talking.

I will get real hot about *stuff*,
Instead of
Staying civil, cool, and composed.

I will die inside,
Instead of
Killing those fears I have sowed.

Don't Break Your Stride

Don't break your stride,
Though the race is long.
Don't desire to hide,
Though your despised face is well-known.

Don't negotiate for your life,
Because the dead have no bargaining power.
Don't live for the minute,
When there are sixty in each hour.

Don't reach for your freedom,
As though it was a handout from another.
Don't compromise through fear,
While hate kills your brother.

Don't curse your blackness
Or utter a sound of regret.
Don't think it to be shameful,
When God is Blacker yet.

Don't break your stride,
Though the race is long.
Don't desire to hide,
Though your despised face is well-known.

World's New Order

Some women will kill for love,
While others would love to kill,
Because men make them swallow
Such big pills.

Men wreck their lives,
And leave them broke,
Or just make babies
That they don't support.

But the world has now changed
From the old to the new.
Where men once ruled,
Women now do.

Judges despise your
Shiftless ways, son.
And your woman is being counseled
On when to use *her gun.*

A Poem Signed "Anonymous"

A Black poet need not write a poem
and sign it "Anonymous."
Unless Anonymous signifies that
He is living in a nation of illiterate children
who refuse to rise above the ignorance of their fathers,
He is just wasting his mind.
To sign a poem Anonymous is also embarrassing.
Kind of like having a not so funny joke
played on you for more than 400 years,
then in the end, when you finally catch on,
you fail to have the last laugh.
Anonymous means "of unknown authorship or origin."
Everyone knows who you are and from whence you come.
You can neither hide nor escape.
At best you could forever wear the mask.
But wearing the mask cannot hide
the deep mental scars of your oppression.
Your scars are what revolutions are made of.
Your scars are revolutionary.
Besides, it's not the poet they want.
They want the apologists to keep the militants in check.
But before this poem suggests that
I am a militant who would not hesitate
to agitate the good white folks . . . .

—Anonymous

Advice

Now to you, my sons, it's time to pass the torch.
Give life everything you have and take as much.
But don't you take anything that is not yours,
This includes money, love, and the other man's girl.
Your living will merge with the direction you claim.
And a few words well-spoken can divert much pain.
A good education will take you a very long way,
for all your heart desires be willing to pay.
Life can be your enemy or life can be your friend,
but life will be honest and never once pretend.
You won't get far without paying your dues,
you will have to take roads you did not choose.
So I tell you these things I know God promotes,
keep your strength and your future has hope.
Understanding is as great as anything on this earth.
In the words of the prophet, "You must commend mirth."
Stay determined like that old stubborn-acting mule,
then stand tall like a mountain that can't be moved.
From your birth until your final days are through,
don't be bad, but always keep the bad ones off you.

Hero

Sammy is a hero and
a veteran of two major wars.
If you think that brother was not tough,
just take a look at his scars.

He lost his heart in Korea,
and his soul in Vietnam.
Although he made it back home,
no one really gives a damn.

Now Sammy is shell shocked
with hardly any mind at all.

(I'm not dying to be no hero, y'all!)

Innocence

I love to watch the pouring rain
and listen to the outbursts of the clouds'
joyful expressions of excitement during
heaven's rehearsal for spring's arrival.
I get lost in life's imaginative serenity,
as I marvel at the Creator's handiwork,
replenishing this wretched earth
so that the meek might inherit something
from that which nature has patiently perfected.
Then I wonder: Are the flowers that bloom
dead souls of Black People who have returned,
as a sign to the children that we shall rise again?

Who cannot understand the patience of the children
in waiting for a sign to rise again?

Nobody Loves Me

Nobody loves me,
And I don't know why.
Guess I'll look for love over yonder—
In the great blue-eyed sky.

"Jesus loves me?"
Oh, what a good lie!
Jesus hasn't heard a word
Since I started to cry.

I'm going to rearrange those lyrics
To that fool child song.
Let me stay black and die,
That's the surest thing going.

You say you love me,
Then tell me why—
You will show love only
Should I suddenly die.

Forever and One Day

When my lover left me,
I wanted to die.
From the top of my balcony,
I said, "Goodbye."

All I could feel
Was the need to die,
Then I opened my eyes
And that was too high.

I placed weights on my ankles
To jump from a bridge,
But the water seemed cold,
On that thought I reneged.

Now I was determined
That I would not choke,
When your lover leaves
Living has little hope.

I bought myself a gun
With nothing more to say,
But who should find me
Being dead this way?

This zest for dying,
I entertained while sad,

Followed the good times
When life wasn't all bad.

I got down on my knees
And began to pray:
Lord, send me a love
That'll come to stay.

Forever and one day!
Forever and one day!

Mother (for Weader Mae)

She wears that old bandana, This Mother of the fields,
Her hope, as with her sweat,
Is to see the earth fulfilled.

Her crown is tightly tied,
Covering ancient civilizations' braids,
But salt is poured in a Mother's eyes,
When God's sun bears no pity for shade.

She wears that old bandana,
Ragged, proud, and beat,
Forever watching and waiting,
For that day when souls will meet.

Forever watching and waiting,
For that day when souls will meet,
With a bandana on her head,
Heaven sleeps at her feet.

A Poem About The Black Woman

How do you begin to begin
a poem about the Black Woman?
And when does it end?
If her poem begins with the wisdom
She possessed in creating the heavens,
and ends with her compassion to form the earth
and all that which exists therein,
it would somehow still offend.
Not because she is personified
with the attributes of God,
But because limitations have been placed
on her handiwork.
The universe is her footstool.
Ancient civilizations have come from her womb.
From her bosom she brings forth the substance of life.
Directing Man to the road of salvation is her pleasure.
All the world shall bow and honor her . . .
Then by her grace a new beginning shall debut.

What I See When You Alone Dream With Me

When you alone dream with me, I can see the horizon over majestic mountains and drink cool waters that continually flow from love's enchanting fountains. Autumn visits on hot summer days, leaves are forever green while devastating winters are neither cold nor mean. Oceans roar with awesome waves, that in times past would have sunk mightier ships, but our little love boat is unaffected, as we sail down a stream of comely beauty that is both straight and narrow, ample room for two but no excess. I feel the warm embrace of your soothing touch that burns like a fire in hell's furnace, yet everything about you is heavenly. You are the divine assurance that washes away a reprobate's sins after communal confession. The only conviction left is that of unabashed fulfillment. I see disagreement, but our biggest quarrel is over who loves whom most. Then night falls and a new dawn sneaks upon us, but the sun still shines because it would dare not set on our love. The only sounds we hear are the echoes of our hearts beating in sync with the confirmation that we are one. Life is bountiful. And because you love like a child with a pure heart, you dare me to love you more today than I did yesterday (like that is possible). And since I, too, have the pure heart of a child, I believe I can cheat ancient wisdom and accept your challenge, all along knowing that I win because I can do the impossible with you. Then you make up an excuse for me and say that the only reason my love is stronger today than it was yesterday is because of the value the Creator adds to our continued existence. And because you know what I like, you throw in some old-time philosophy that you say your mother told you will make a good man think: "What a joy living brings when you don't demand perfection." But my simple response should make you think (my mother talked to me, too): "True beauty can only be seen by those whose hearts negotiate its sight." You always told me that I have 20/20 vision because I make the right decisions.

Although I must trust that right has something to do with sight, I do know that dreaming is a most wonderful thing to do. Having reassured you, you also dream and now can see what I see, when you alone dream with me.

Vision of a Future Past

I've seen young men who grimly appear
older than their years would ever suggest.
I've seen young girls who often abuse
their youth with seductive ways of dress.
I've seen children hide their many sins
through loving parents who would rescue.
I've seen the same love sentenced parents
to lives of shame the way only love can do.
I've seen a judicial system show its disdain
for children and inhumanely lock them down.
I've seen a society look at results in horror
then hide and pledge to never come around.
I've seen a world that gives then takes back
the hopes and dreams of a people in distrust.
I've seen the destruction that inevitably occurs
when freedom has real meaning for everyone but us.

Child to Father

When a father forsakes and abandons his young,
from where will their true understanding come?
Are they condemned to hell and free to burn
like illiterate children who will never learn?
Will they temper love with a feverish soul,
and precipitate death should they grow old?
Will they see the world through the eyes of hate,
or just curse God for his cruel mistake?
Will they enter a race that finishes last,
confined to a lifetime of wearing the mask?
Will the appeal of success make them procrastinate,
never a winner because they sleep too late?
Will your son walk tall like a mighty proud man,
or wander through life seeking a helping hand?
Will your daughter spoil her babies with sour milk,
and just blame her mother while passing the guilt?
Will children dare to dream and keep the shrine,
or inherit the legacy of dying before their time.

In Remembrance Of

Your keeper has a hobby of
Treating people like playing with soldering toys.
Indiscriminately he maneuvers
Old men, women, and young boys
All around the world
To make his life better.
He takes your life,
You are buried with his medal.

Black Love

There is no love in this world
More valuable than Black Love.
None that penetrates as deep
With as much Spirit and Soul.

There is no gem in the earth as precious,
Or as beautiful when petrified.
Black Love is earth's diamond,
The image of forever for the world to delight.
It is the eternal sun of the heavens.

There is no God that can deny His allegiance
To Black Love undaunted,
Though scattered across the wilderness,
And Troubled.

In fact, there is no nothing
That can avoid becoming something,
When Black Love works
In touch with each other.

Wish

For once,
I wish I were so understood
until misunderstanding consults with me
on the proper way to handle conflict.
Or adversity charges me with guardianship
over elevating the consciousness of my adversaries.

I would perform miracles!

I would first restore sight to Lady Liberty,
so that she could stop blaming legal blindness
for her sightless injustices.
Next, I would raise a beloved People
from their dead-like sleep.

Then all the world would know
the true meaning of equality.
On that day,
the same rock you dropped on me
would land on you.

The Lost Generation

School is seen as such a doggone bore,
For adolescent Black boys over four.
Instead of books they carry loaded guns
And kill their teachers for failing some.

The rules are mean from the distant shore,
Little minds are locked out forevermore.
The States are marveling at great results.
Little children are prosecuted as adults.

Wake up! Wake up!

Make Footsteps

Make footsteps with feet that are tired and sore.
Walk one mile in shoes never broken in before.
Dare to be different and let your humanity remain.
Life is for the living and longevity is your gain.

Make footsteps as you thirst across the hot desert,
Or stop along the shores when your aching feet hurt.
Whether anyone knows of your plight or who you are,
Your journey is a measure of the traveler's heart.

Make footsteps of self-love to take along and befriend.
And to yourself you must remain true until the very end.
Live your dreams and never be discouraged by their cost,
Winners rejoice in winning and are strengthened in loss.

Make footsteps unto the hearts of a nation in dire need.
As the flowers wither and die, bring forth brand-new seeds.
Take the children by their hands and begin to teach.
They are one and the same and as one you must give each.

Make footsteps along roads that are desolate and bare.
Let your bold signature state that you have been there.
Make footsteps with instructions on how to do the same.
When the wind blows the dust away you have left a name.

Always Remember The Children

Always remember the children
and pray they will never forget.
Remember the meaning of love
and show them what love begets.

Remember the minds of children,
though innocent this might seem.
Children will curse hopelessness,
when someone defers their dreams.

Remember this lost generation,
before they decide to be found.
You can't run from the madness,
only pray they won't come around.

Always remember the children,
and they will give their best.
Remove burdens and limitations;
provide them tools for success.

Remember the children when teaching,
and teach with love that understands.
Let them live and enjoy their youth,
they become respected women and men.

Always remember the precious children,
before the chance has come and gone.

When the children are soon forgotten,
there will be destruction in the home.

This Too Is Poetry

Poetry is defined as "the productions of the poet."
The poet is, thus, responsible for employing
his proverbial license to enlighten
and elevate the consciousness of his people.
The poet must give meaning to life.
This is to say that the poet must not own shame,
unless it can be found in his failures to attempt.
The poet is simultaneously the vision for the future's past
and the past's evolving future.
Poetry is his movement.
It is his movement from present conditions
to a future time of paradoxical uncertainty.
Poetry is the prologue of some past development.
Most Black People are poetic.
Poetry is finding and remembering.
Poetic is losing and forgetting.
Poetry is rhythmic.
Although life does not always rhyme,
It is nonetheless rhythmic.
Being poetic is to be in a state of becoming.
Poetry is life's compulsion to arrive.
Black People are just beginning to understand
that they must first become in order to arrive.
If we refuse to differentiate between
the will and defiance it takes to become and arrive,
then Black People are poetry, though be it in motion.
But a careful examination of their mindset

will conclusively reveal that Black People are poetic.
But this, too, is poetry.
The poet will cross great gulfs
when there is a chance he might capitalize
on his courageous experience.
The poetic one will passively approach a stream
then run and hide when he sees
his enemy's face reflected therein.
And I am compelled to believe that
This, too, is poetry.
Can you see how "run and hide"
rhymes with "genocide"?

About the Author

Andrew Marshall, Jr. B.A, M.A. was born and raised in Columbus, Georgia, and also attended Claflin Elementary School, a formerly segregated public school that is approximately 145 years old. Claflin Elementary School consisted of grades kindergarten through sixth. Coincidentally, the Author's father, Andrew Marshall, Sr., also attended Claflin as a child growing up in Columbus. Andrew Marshall, Jr., was a student in the last sixth grade class at Claflin, immediately prior to Columbus, Georgia experiencing mandated integration of this Nation's public-school systems.

In June 1976, after completing his junior year, the Author graduated from high school. In December of the same year, when he was still 17 years old, Andrew enlisted in the United States Marine Corps (USMC). Prior to leaving for Boot Camp, he made an attempt to count every house and/or lots (where a home had once stood) that he could remember having lived during his upbringing. Subsequently, he counted 13 different home locations. After conferring with an older sister on this number, that sister told him that he had missed two other houses. The Author is capable of recalling practically every day of his life.

Andrew Marshall, Jr. had a once in a lifetime experience when he met and conversed with one of history's greatest literary giants of poetry, Miss Gwendolyn Brooks, who was the first African American to win the Pulitzer Prize for her book Annie Allen (poetry). Reverently, this chance meeting and brief discussions with Miss Gwendolyn Brooks have been the motivation for some of Andrew Marshall, Jr., more poignant allegorical and metaphorical writings (satirical as well). Additionally, this Author has historically embraced the writings of Langston Hughes, Paul Lawrence Dunbar, along with many of the other notable Harlem Renaissance Writers. With respect to this literary field of endeavors, Andrew Marshall, Jr. has read and/or attempted to analyze the works of many other authors, whether contemporary or historical.

Andrew Marshall, Jr., graduated in 1983 with honors from Bethune-Cookman University (formerly, "Bethune-Cookman College"), an HBCU or Historically Black College or University. After graduating from Bethune-Cookman, Andrew Marshall, Jr. completed a Master's of Science degree in Human Resources Management and Development at National Louis University. He retired from the United States Federal Government. He is a member of Kappa Alpha Psi Fraternity, Incorporated.

Index

A Love Deferment 97

A Poem About The Black Woman 144

A Poem Signed "Anonymous" 136

Advice 137

Along the Way 30

Always Remember The Children 154

America 28

APES Running Free 107

Beautiful 117

Beautiful, Children 69

Black Love 150

Black People Got Sores 6

Bridge 129

Caring 87

Censored 91

Child to Father 148

Civil Rights Movement 109

Color-blind 21

Commencing 88

Complicit 121

Conferred 110

Conscientious Divider 47

Count Sheep Before Falling Asleep 108

Dashing 125

Death Notice 59

Don't Break Your Stride 134

Don't Doubt the Prayer's Answers 96

Dust-off 57

Elevation 14

Escape 19

Eyes 36

Fantasy 80

Father to Daughter 76

First Person Plural 105

Flamboyant 100

Forever and One Day 141

Four-Leaf Clovers 75

Freedom 20

Generation Conflict 130

Give Me My Flowers Now	62
Hard Times	12
Heritage	101
Hero	138
High on that Sun	52
Holding Down	18
Home Economics	99
Honeybee	74
Hurricane, Eye	51
I Am That Man	131
I Must Set History Straight!	3
I Pray for You, Two	103
I Pray You Sleep Well Tonight	29
If We Are Not the Last to Laugh	26
In My Eyes	42
In Remembrance Of	23, 149
Ingredients for Love	98
Innocence	139
Inseparable	11
Instead Of	133

Interpretation and Response 4

It 79

It is Written 39

Just Imagine What My Mule Could Be Doing 123

Just Wait 10

Last Minute 13

Lead Me But Don't Be Miss-LEAD 68

Lights Off 17

Like a Water Breaking 61

Lone Soldering 102

Love 27

Love Me With Your Lust for Love 58

Luck 71

Make Footsteps 153

Memory 34

Mother 143

Mother Furious 119

My Sins Hasn't The Taste for Gin 65

New Love 86

Nobody Loves Me 140

Northern Hospitality 15

Not on Your Own Time 120

Nowhere Home 25

Old Shade Tree 31

One Proud Nation of Prouds 43

Openly Booked 56

Overdosage 93

Paradox 8

Praying Butterfly Prey 48

Prophetic 35

Props Proper Properly 78

Punctuation Markings 124

Pyromaniac 84

Question with Nothing Answer 24

Rebel 5

Refund 106

Retolled2Death 66

Revolution 37

Same Warning Against Your Other Warnings 73

Self-Medicating 64

So, Tardy of Time 115

Stir the Pot 113

Stoned 118

Stubborn 85

Synonymous With The "N" in NAACP 50

Tainted Gold 89

Tap Dancers 112

The Black Set Back 127

The Golden Shovel 53

The Great Fuss 77

The Life Love Left for Dead 54

The Lost Generation 152

The Making of Me 70

The Traveler 2

The Verdict 92

The Word 128

There is No Second Hand on the Ticked-off Clock 81

There Was Always One Open Option Left Open After the Last Option Wasn't Close 114

They Sing 16

This Too Is Poetry 156

Three Tenets for Understanding Democracy	22
To Hell with Aches	104
To Hell with Nothing for All	122
Tour for a Black Soldier	38
Trapped	90
Turning Point	45
Two Faces	46
Unmasking	94
US is Not "WE" Friendly	116
Vision of a Future Past	147
WE The Feed for The FED	67
Well-Watered Years	55
What Do You People Want?	7
What Hope Has the Race?	32
What I See When You Alone Dream With Me	145
Window Shopping	126
Wish	151
Without Cause	9
Words That Sound Like Freedom	1
World's New Order	135

You are a Tomorrow's Baby 82

You, Too, is America, Too 72

Your Knowledge Wealth 95